T0368492

PSYCHOLOGY WITHIN THE CONTEXT OF PSYCHIATRY

CLOSING THE TRANSLATIONAL GAP

AMY TWILEGAR

WestBow Press books may be ordered through booksellers or by contacting:

WestBow Press
A Division of Thomas Nelson & Zondervan
1663 Liberty Drive
Bloomington, IN 47403
www.westbowpress.com
844-714-3454

ISBN: 979-8-3850-2490-2 (sc)
ISBN: 979-8-3850-3232-7 (hc)
ISBN: 979-8-3850-2491-9 (e)

Library of Congress Control Number: 2024908974

Print information available on the last page.

WestBow Press rev. date: 8/26/2024

WESTBOW
PRESS®
A DIVISION OF THOMAS NELSON
& ZONDERVAN

Acknowledgements

I would like to thank all of my family, friends and loved ones in the production and support of this book; without them this would not have been possible. Most importantly, however, I give thanks to my Lord Jesus Christ; without Him, my life would not have been possible. I am very grateful to present this work.

FOREWORD

The fields of Psychology and Psychiatry are founded on the assessment and treatment practices for mental health and treating disorders, characterized by significant impairments to an individual's cognitive functioning, emotion regulation and behavior; causing distress to the afflicted individual, these functional impairments significantly impact the lives of those who suffer from, and manage, these dysfunctional states. The current DSM-5 (Diagnostic and Statistical Manual for Mental Disorders, 5th edition), portends that diagnoses are based on rigid structures of criteria by which clinicians must follow in order to assess patients; in cases where medical intervention is necessary for treatment protocol, these patients are then referred to specialists in order to treat the individual with medical care.

Standard treatment plans maintain adherence to guidelines which must be followed within each profession; however, research integration from an interdisciplinary approach sheds new light on the utility in reconstructing these structured variables confounded within these criteria sets; namely, that of ADHD with regard to age of onset and predisposition of certain traits. When considering variables outside the scope of widely accepted and currently practiced assessment measures, new conceptualizations emerge through extenuated research to offer alternative perspectives for labeling when it comes to developmental effects. Though difficult to measure in laboratory settings, the early environmental influences such as parental caregiving relationships lends valuable insight to developmental factors in considering adult onset of ADHD.

TABLE OF CONTENTS

I. Psychology Within the Context of Psychiatry

The fields of psychology and psychiatry often are misconstrued as having a ubiquitous perspective on psychopathological traits. Beyond the scope of their profession, there seems to be a need for mapping the theoretical frameworks, such as clinical inferences, onto biological data, such as fMRI scans, thereby linking tangible evidence of brain activity patterns with regard to psychopathological constructs. This, in turn, provides valuable cross-reference evidence to further examine the confluence in labeling when considering the underlying mechanisms for psychological disorders. Within the context of ADHD, namely, with particular insight to adult onset of symptomatology, thorough analyses of literary publications and research studies renders a more critical evaluative view.

Emerging evidence suggests an ongoing struggle to fully understand the paradoxical inferences surrounding the benchmark qualitative features in regards to labeling ADHD, defined by the latest Diagnostic and Statistical Manual for Mental Disorders (DSM-5.1, last reviewed in May 2013) as a disorder which must be present in childhood (American Psychiatric Association, 2013). With a more critical look at the history and profligates of theories, however, it seems necessary to take a closer look at the complex interplay between factors which constitute developmental interferences, such as parent-child dynamics, as well as environmental disparities within the home environment settings. Relationships with primary caregivers developed through the early years formed through critical phases of development and the predispositioned vulnerabilities imposed as risk factors on abused children suffering from abuse and/or neglect are further explored. The higher comorbidities with other mental illnesses, as well as predispositioned psychophysiological factors, thus need a greater level of integration in quantitative analyses considering the limited criteria-based factors in qualitatively defining the parametric standards in labeling ADHD. With respect to self-informant measures and case history reports, it becomes clear the need to consider reconstructed variables which define ADHD to this day.

The rigid structure criteria for labeling ADHD, particularly with regard to adult populations, calls for need of revision when considering predisposition roles. Abusive home environments, as well as reactant trends, lends greater flexibility in understanding the detrimental effects of abusive environments, and thus highlights the need for restructuring the confining variables for this mental disease. With particular emphasis on the role of fear in developing brains, it becomes clear at the level of biological setback this salient factor infers. Contextual variables and individual differences reflect the variance observed in statistical modeling approaches; however, when controlling for demographic features in addition to reporter-related variables, trends among self-report measures begin to emerge. Though current diagnostic criteria seem to bridge consideration factors such as adult onset of ADHD, the overarching theories are seemingly still reluctant in deviating from definitive confines. One reason for this adherence to diagnostic nomenclature may be largely, in part, due to parent- vs. individual, subjective reporting across age groups, as well as limited clinical testing regarding past history events (Bieleninik et al., 2023). As such, it seems important to recognize the correlations among self-report measures when considering patterns among those afflicted and the related variables for symptoms as well as case history when identifying these trends.

Further analyses reveal specified attentional networks related to performance tests. Recent research conducted by Bieleninik et al. (2023) reveals findings among school-aged children and their respective cognitive functioning performances with regard to alertness and executive functioning. Though significant differences were observed between those diagnosed with ADHD and those at high risk of developmental delays in childhood, these measures highlight differential performances compared to normative groups. Reasons for this discernment, however, may reflect the treatment variables of valuable asset when considering the differential factors between those clinically diagnosed, in comparison to proneness risk groups. Additionally, when compared to adult populations, evidence reflects an observer-specific deviation due to parent- vs. individual reports. Nevertheless, studies show relational contrast between groups for ADHD-like symptomatology expressions and those categorized in normative groups, showing attentional capacity differentiations across frontal-striatal-cerebellar network activation patterns in the brain. Studies have called for further necessary research among such populations beyond the scope of these measures to further consider more critical evaluation beyond factors for attentional control; in addition to response selection and inhibition, it also seems pertinent to consider context-dependent measures, such as home environment and age of onset, in addition to confounding variables such as predispositioned traits.

To further exemplify the need to consider context-dependent variables, I contend that other factors should be critically evaluated, such as exposure to abusive environments in the early years; as such, this may set the stage for development of vulnerabilities in attentional limitations and brain networking, which upon recall in case history studies have shown to correlate strongly with negative cognitive trends. In retrospect, I present a critically acclaimed literature research review on such measures, as well as a personally conducted pseudo analytical study with which to assess other surveyed variables to consider regarding supplementary factors for further evaluating the etiological and progressive significance in the development of ADHD. Lastly, I aim to close the translational gap between the two subdisciplines of psychology, by mapping the theoretical frameworks onto biological data such as fMRI scans, to amalgamate the two discrepant fields and unify a more correspondent understanding of the biological bases for ADHD, as well as the relative precursors which set the stage for further developmental disabilities in cognitive functioning and high-risk factors to be considered. Early relationship influences, shown to cascade through age-specific critical years, have been found to play key roles in the development for attentional capacities and emotional control. In the event that abusive relationships are experienced in the early years, maladjusted patterns to these negative events may thereby elicit behavioral anomalies likely seen throughout later stages and impose aversive consequential effects. Attentional networks may therefore be compromised in the developing brain, thus rendering the need for further review regarding conventional categorical constructs for ADHD in adulthood, given these factorial constraints.

II. Diagnostic Tools for Practitioners

i. Diagnostic Assessment

The American Psychological Association defines clinical assessments as the systematic evaluation and measurement of psychological, biological, and social factors in a person presenting a possible psychological disorder (American Psychological Association, 2018). An array of methods and instruments (measures) are used by mental health practitioners, typically psychologists, to evaluate an individual's functioning in multiple areas and to inform and facilitate decisions or recommendations intended to improve functioning in one or more areas (Carlson, 2016). Good rapport must be made with key principles such as honesty, integrity, and empathy to build good physician-patient relationships and communication. In doing so, a sense of trust and honesty is made to establish professional and quality care. A patient's "story" is heard and through unbiased viewpoints, appropriate treatment regimens are made suitable to the needs of the patient, and a program is then made to help the patient with the psychologist, tailored to the individual's needs. The DSM-5, currently used today, is the tool by which psychologists make informed decisions on patient diagnoses, acting as a guideline to assess patients' mental health. The DSM undergoes revisions as necessary throughout the years, as diagnoses may change throughout the course of definitive adjustments made through research findings. If deemed necessary, clinicians may refer patients to specialists such as psychiatrists, should medical intervention be recommended by the psychologist in their diagnostic assessment.

ii. Psychiatric Evaluation

The American Psychological Association defines psychiatric evaluations as assessments, based on present problems and symptoms, of an individual's biological, mental, and social functioning, which may or may not result in a diagnosis of a mental illness (American Psychological Association, 2018). Psychiatrists rarely show empathy in their observations and evaluations, as the main purpose is to confirm diagnoses and formulate proper treatment plans (Rosburg, von Allmen, Langewitz, Weber, Bunker, & Langewitz, 2019). Unlike psychologists, the role of psychiatrists is to confirm diagnoses and formulate appropriate treatment plans, oftentimes implementing prescription medication, in order to help the patient overcome their illness and relieve symptoms the patient presents and alleviate the ailments being suffered by the patient at that time.

III. RESEARCH ANALYSES

Though the constructs for anxiety and empathy have shown to be negatively correlated, much emphasis is needed for further re-assessment of anxious individuals in terms of comorbid traits. Anxious individuals tend to focus their attentional resources toward internalized stress affecting relationships; although this highlights the importance of self-other disconnect, it is also noteworthy to explore the disconnect they may also harbor within. Through a series of surveyed individuals filling out self-report questionnaires, the belief that depression as a paradoxical spectral quality to colligate anxiety was assessed. Though anxiety and empathy were found to be negatively correlated, it was believed that anxiety and depression, in contrast, were positively correlated. The following set of studies conducted and findings presented reveal a significant positive correlation between those with tendencies to feel anxious and those who tend to experience depressive states; a meta-analytical evaluation of these pseudoscientific analyses is presented for review.

Anxiety and Empathy: A Correlational Analysis
by
Amy Twilegar
University of the Rockies
PSY 6400 Quantitative Research Design and Methods
Professor: Dr. L. G. Olson-Davidson, Ph. D.
November, 2011

Abstract

The goal of the current study is to examine the relationship between anxiety and empathy ability. It is hypothesized that there is a measurable difference between those that have anxiety and those who exhibit empathic ability. To measure such constructs, we take a multidimensional approach to considering cognitive perspective-taking abilities in relation to the capacity to feel for others and exhibit their frame of reference, or state of mind.

Chapter 1
Introduction

The ability to show empathy is a complex interactional process that entails a multitude of factors, ranging from cognitive perspective-taking to emotional concern. The literature contains a long history of definitions describing typically one dimension or both for the construct of empathy; however, to gain a full understanding of the complex psychological measure, it is necessary to integrate social as well as neuroscientific analysis in determining the underlying causes and function of emotions.

As a complex social species, humans are adapted to meet their environmental demands by responding effectively and communicating needs. The behavioral system then interprets the messages based on affective responses, making evaluative judgments and cognitive appraisals. Traditionally thought of as shyness around strangers or nervousness to perform or give a speech, researchers are now recognizing the scope of functional impairments impeded by social anxiety. Attachment insecurities may arise in response to maladaptive coping strategies to stress experienced in the environment; such maladjusted psychological constructs such as anxiety then limit the social competence in later years and relationships.

In recent years, research has turned its focus on the role of emotions in shaping the neural pathways that regulate behavior. Cognitive and emotional processing affects the ways that perceptions and memories are formed in the mind, with variation accounting for individual differences and contextual effects.

Chapter 2
Literature Review

As a social species, human beings are adapted to meet the changing conditions of the environment, while at the same time striving to meet the challenges they face between each other. Early theorists speculated the role of emotions in human experience, attributing their affective abilities to convey useful social information; measuring the complex organization and interactions between factors, one must correlate variables to reveal patterns of relationships (Frankfort-Nachmias & Nachmias, 2008). Evolutionary perspectives highlight the importance of primary-process circuits for emotional stimuli to produce memory-laden constructs representing evaluative appraisals (Snowden, 2003).

The primitive brain is organized according to these approach-avoidance strategies in order to ensure quick access to available neural connections, informing the organism whether or not it is safe to explore their environment (Bowlby, 1982). Other key elements of emotional content compromising this meaning-based system may include, but are not limited to, resource extraction such as food or comfort in times of need, as well as safety from harm. Affective representations are thus formed according to the mental schemata associated with such events, aimed at protecting the species from injurious conditions and avoiding threat or harm. As humans have progressed to utilize these primitive social-emotional circuits to activate communicative messages past the early years, these systems become integrated into more complex modes of interactive exchange. Advances in neuroscientific research offer valuable insight to behavioral systems, to explain the nature of emotional affectivity within the context of social bonds (Pelligra, 2011).

As a social species, one of the most basic human drives is the desire to be accepted by others (Baumeister & Leary, 1995). Social exclusion and rejection can have a negative impact on psychological and behavioral outcomes, from emotional disengagement to destructive choices signaling self-defeat (Krishnan & Nestler, 2008). Devoid sense of fulfillment and deflated self-esteem characterize the negative self-representations which sets exclusion apart from rejection. Social exclusion has been shown to lead to avoidance of self-awareness, as self-reflection of others' negative thoughts elicit feelings of emotional distress; transient states of anxiety therefore promote a shifting of attention, away from thoughts of rejection to avoid sustainable injury by suppression of pain (Twenge, Cataneser & Baumeister, 2003).

Allaying painful experiences can generate a host of negative effects, on mental faculties and social dysfunctions (Shaver, Segev, & Mikulincer, 2011). Maladaptive coping strategies in efforts to regain a sense of control may lead to ineffective behavioral system patterns as a function of psychosocial adjustment. Developmental consequences of the inherent bases of psychological pain have been shown to affect relational constructs, and the tendencies to offer support; prior psychoanalytic theorists address the limitations of suppressed experiences to contribute unconscious motivations to self-protective defenses (Cassidy & Kobak, 1998; Bowlby, 1982).

Empirical studies investigating proactive social behavior, characterized by offering help to those in need, looked at middle school and adolescent students, comparing different forms of insecurities and aggression (Culotta & Goldstein, 2008). After controlling for gender and race, investigators found that jealousy was a strong predictor of prosocial tendencies and aggression, with respect to relational but not physical acts; the authors also found social anxiety to be predictive of prosocial behavior. Mikulincer & Shaver (2007) found this relational feature of the system to be a primary influence on others to attain one's goals. The behavioral system's attempts to gain acceptance and control reflect intrusive anxieties and constant worry in fulfilling the need to avoid feelings of self-defeat (Shaver, Segev, & Mikulincer, 2011).

The physiological reactivity experienced as a consequence of anxiety elicits heightened states of arousal measured by heart rate accelerations (Cacioppo & Sandman, 1978). According to the literature, this internal state of distress may reflect self-perceived threats, initiating a cascade of inner focusing on emotional insecurities (Eisenberg, 2009). In a series of studies examining the effects of sympathy and personal distress on emotional comforting to others, sympathetic responding was found to relate more with decelerations in heart rate activity, evidence for externally-stimulated responses across children and adults (Eisenberg, Fabes, Bustamante, Mathy, Miller, & Lindholm, 1988; Eisenberg et al., 1988).

A further distinction to make for measures of emotional responding would delineate self- and other-oriented reactions, with which expressions are motivated by differential experiences. Emotional contagion, which can be witnessed between infants' crying as distress signals, lacks the psychological maturity for awareness of self from other (Scheler, 1973). Affective empathy, on the other hand, presupposes self-other awareness; however, this distinction is preliminary to emotional reactions devoted to another's state (Hoffman, 2000). Sympathy involves responding to the distressed in comforting ways without relating emotionally (Eisenberg, 2000), whereas personal distress involves subjective relatedness but is self-oriented (Batson, Fultze, & Shoenrade, 1987).

Empathy is a construct which describes the cognitive and emotional aspects to feeling the distress of others, while expressing concern in appropriate ways. A series of historical perspectives outlines the basic framework for which the concept of empathy can be measured (Hein & Singer, 2010). Hoffman (1981) suggests empathy to be an appropriate affective response closely associated with another's experience; given the self-other distinction is clearly defined, distress is then codified for differing levels of introspection. Empathic bases for distress involve adopting an affective stance related to the emotional experience of another, to share its mutual effects; sympathetic distress, conversely, arises out of concern for another's well-being (Hein & Singer, 2010). Though not mutually exclusive, aspects of empathy and sympathy diverge on the tendency to help others.

Prosocial behavior has been shown to correlate positively with sympathy, and negatively with personal distress (Eisenberg & Miller, 1987). To better understand these concepts, recent personality research compares empathic concern to agreeableness and personal distress to neuroticism (Mooradian, Davis, & Matzler, 2011). Sympathy may represent concern for another's welfare or simply rely on perspective-taking abilities; however, the invasive consequence of neuroticism predisposes a vulnerability to experience negative emotions.

Building on previous literature correlating self-reported empathy scores to prosocial giving behaviors (Davis, Mitchell, Hall, Lothert, Snapp, & Meyer, 1999; Ben-Ner, Kong, & Putterman, 2004; Ben-Ner & Halldorsson, 2010), choices in doing so are shown to be influenced by agreeableness as well as trust; in contrast, reciprocity is influenced by perspective-taking abilities (Gunnthorsdottir, McCabe, & Smith, 2002). Internal representations of others' intentions and emotional states therefore serve to function as indicators of unconscious motivations (Preston & de Waal, 2002). In this sense, self- and other-oriented behaviors may converge on prosocial motives driven by empathic displays, in efforts to maintain positive interactions as well as avoid feelings of shame or guilt (Pelligra, 2011). Alternatively, self-regarding behaviors may serve to maximize external rewards, whereas other-regarding behaviors may influence decisions to avoid harming others, in turn avoiding guilt. These prosocial tendencies enhanced by empathic abilities suggests the more individuals show affective concern, the more likely they will behave altruistically, regardless of whether it is genuine (Singher & Fehr, 2005).

Anticipating the needs of others and fulfilling expected roles can evade negative reactions, emotions and conflict, while promoting a positive self-image (Pelligra, 2011). Other-oriented behaviors may not always benefit from compliance, however, in cases where the cost is injurious to the self. Misdirected expressions of anger at unjust treatment or feeling devalued can provoke internal conflict, resulting in anxiety from internalizing fears or aggressive impulses (Summers, 2005). Empathic concerns for others may prohibit confrontations to avoid distress, which may only turn these negative emotions inward, leaving one to face the battle within. In this sense, self-defeating behaviors may arise from social compliance; avoiding pain elicitation in others may serve to intensify pain in the self. The inability to effectively convey frustrations at the cost of sensitivity and concern for others indicates the ability to feel and show empathy; however, the self and other still seem dependently intertwined (Summers, 2005).

Developmental approaches address early relational experiences as opportunities for fostering personal growth, interactions which promote self and other representations from which to learn social skills (Thompson, 2010). These mental representations, known as internal working models, organize attachment relationships and provide a cognitive framework for conceptualizing the world. Specifically, these mental models provide the developing child a sense of security, enhanced emotion understanding, expectations for social behavior, and emotion regulation strategies (Thompson, 2010). Attachment theory, as proposed by Mikulincer, Shaver, & Rom (2011), is centered on affect regulation within the context of close relationships. The focus of current research highlights the importance of perceived security in providing internal working models for emotional stability, exploration and learning. Investigating the effects of security priming through implicit and explicit measures, findings revealed subliminal cues of attachment figures sparked creativity in problem-solving, whereas explicit recalling was mediated by insecurities.

With regard to empathy in adolescence and adulthood, attachment security was found to enhance emotional concern, compassion, altruism, gratitude, and forgiveness (Shaver & Mikulincer, 2012). Shown in previous years to be related to prosocial and other-oriented behaviors, patterns of attachment and prosocial motives have included morality to examine choice behaviors. Attachment insecurities for anxiety and avoidance were shown to impinge on prosocial motives, emotions and behavior; anxiety, in particular, encouraged moral choices over ego defense. Within the frame of interpersonal contexts, therefore, attachment security induction was shown to elicit prosocial moral choices in the place of defensive morality for individuals anxiously-attached (Shaver & Mikulincer, 2012).

Other studies have focused on the role of other individual differences such as gender, race and age. High school students were investigated with regard to gender, building on the expected finding that empathy and prosocial behavior were correlated (Barr & D'Alessandro, 2007). Comparing a large, traditional public high school with a small alternative school for validity purposes, investigators found that males' greater positive perceptions of school culture were related to greater empathy but not prosocial behavior; thus, gender was the moderating variable, rather than age. Findings revealed emotional concern as a factor of empathy was related more to positive perceptions of peer relationships than to other dimensional social components (Barr & D'Alessandro, 2007); In a similar study comparing young children and peers, helping behavior and offerings were shown to exchange most frequently among peer dyads; compared with non-friend behaviors, findings suggest friendships influence prosocial tendencies and reciprocity (Fujisawa, Kutsukake, & Hasegawa, 2008).

In a cross-comparison between children and adolescents for moral choices, six-year-old children were rated longitudinally on prosocial behavior and sympathy by observers (Malti, Gummerum, Keller,

& Buchmann, 2009). Greater sympathy predicted prosocial behavior, particularly when accompanied by low moral motivation, characterized by emotional attributions and moral reasoning. Findings suggest children adhere to the validity of moral norms set by society as rules which govern behavior; this idea further emphasizes the role of cognitive influence in shaping children's moral choices.

Parental factors also have been identified in perceived need support offered differentially by contributing figures (Miklikowska, Sonens, & Duriez, 2011). Parental need support has shown positive effects on both sons and daughters for adolescent development of perspective-taking abilities; maternal need support, however, has only shown effective development for empathic concern in daughters only. Eisenberg (2006) lends credit to parental support for correlations found with empathy, when explaining these findings within the context of social learning theory. In this view, Eisenberg contends that children are provided opportunities to learn from and experience perspective-taking and emotional concern for others, fostering an optimal setting for development. Attachment theory, in addition, posits parental support is the mechanism by which children learn social and interpersonal skills, strengthening empathic development even further (Bowlby, 1980; Hoffman, 2000; Laible et al., 2004; Sroufe & Fleeson, 1986; van der Mark et al., 2002).

Although secure attachment provided by caregiver need support is beneficial to cognitive and emotional growth, empathic abilities are further reinforced by the identification to a security-enhancing figure (Miklikowsa, Soenens, & Duriez, 2011). The capacity to develop sensitive ways of responding to those in need and fostering a sense of independence adapted to coping with stress elucidates the security perceived and carried through to later intimate relationships. Although the role of parental support figures is beneficial to the developing children, there may inherently be subtle flaws in this practice; whereas fathers may contribute socialization for adolescents' cognitive abilities in perspective-taking, mothers may primarily be involved in affect regulation. These themes follow gender role orientations theory, in which males are socialized for masculine traits, such as power and dominance, where females are assumed to possess feminine qualities such as passivity and dependence (Bem, 1984, 1993; Collins et al., 1993; Coltrane, 1998). Traditional gender norms set expectations in the child's and adolescent's minds, predisposing sets of normative standards of behavior for which differing roles are expected to assume.

Social constructs are learned entities from environmental interactions, often reinforced by parental influences which are socialized implicitly (Miklikowska, Soenens, & Duriez, 2011). With cultural differences negligible, gendered behaviors have been shown to develop from environmental and parental influences, as individual differences for attachment securities affect behavior. Internal working models of supportive caregivers can serve to buffer the effects of stress, and these mental constructs become increasingly complex with age; similarly, gender differences increase as a function of time. Helping behavior and prosocial tendencies such as sympathetic relating to others may reflect a move from self-oriented motivations to other-oriented regard. Hoffman (2000) supports this view, contending that children become increasingly other-oriented as they mature.

Attachment insecurities can have equally negative effects, as approach and avoidance behavioral systems adapt to maladjusted ways of coping to environmental stress (Shaver, Segev, & Mikulincer, 2011). Personality trait variables may reflect these negative influences, shaping qualities such as neuroticism, predisposing a vulnerability to experience negative emotions (Samuel, Clark, Simms, Levesley, & Widiger, 2010). Attachment insecurities for avoidance struggle to maintain emotional distance, though these individuals share negative self-perceptions and mental models of the self and others along with maladjusted coping strategies common to anxiety. Both attachment anxiety and avoidance have emotional dysfunction in relationships, and these negative attributes not only carry into future relationships, but often accompany social rejection in the meantime. Given the evidence findings throughout the literature, anxiety is shown to negatively impact empathic abilities toward others in need.

Functional magnetic resonance imaging (fMRI; Decety & Jackson, 2004) is a neuroimaging technique to observe activation patterns of the neurobiological mechanisms underlying cognitive perspective-taking abilities. Evidence reveals correlations between empathy-related constructs and specific neural activity patterns, further validating the use of empathy questionnaires.

Gazzola, Aziz-Sadeh, & Keysers (2006) found mirror neuron activation levels in the auditory cortex for performing behavioral motor movements and listening to similar activities were stronger in those who scored higher on Davis' IRI measures for cognitive perspective-taking abilities. Additionally, select brain regions involved in information processing of attention and awareness to pain perception and motor circuits have been shown to strongly correlate with the Empathic Concern subscale; these associations suggest inter-individual differences modulate the effects of affective empathy (Lang, Yu, Markl, Muller, & Kotchoubey, 2011).

Lamm, Batson, & Decety (2007) found correlational activation patterns for the right putamen, left posterior/middle insula, anterior medial cingulated cortex, and left cerebellum between these neural networks and Baron-Cohen & Wheelright's (2004) EQ measures. The Empathy Quotient scaled measurement has been shown to have a high test-retest reliability rate between periods of one-year intervals, whose subscales for "empathic concern" and "perspective-taking" are strongly correlated to show concurrent validity (Lawrence, 2004).

Chapter 3
Methodology

The test battery consisting of empathy measures ranges from emotional experience to expression, and diverges between cognitive and emotional dimensions. Pro-social behavior is merely implied in questionnaires, as motivational forces underlying the desire to help others in need are more consistent with the goal in this study. Students who display the desire to respond empathically to others who they perceive to be in need are thus more adaptive and adjusted psychologically for social interaction. The attachment measures may indicate the role of parental influence in shaping these cognitive and empathic constructs; thus, the role of cultural and social identity is shown to play a huge part in determining behavioral trends.

Self-report inventories for adolescent personality development of empathic abilities are given to students, in the form of electronic database scoring and record-keeping. Parents are given paper-and-ink copies to fill out, in attempts to reduce apprehension in participation based on unfamiliar methods or biases. Computer-based appraisals are then measured to determine their results. Case history information and attachment style results are then compared to determine the effect of past experiences on current emotional and cognitive constructs and interaction processes.

The Multiphasic Questionnaire for Emotional Empathy (MEE; Mehrabian & Epstein, 1972) defines empathy in the context of emotional reactivity and affective responsivity. A single score is measured for the empathy as a single scale. Negligibly small effect found between empathic accuracy and affective empathy subscales but no other effects were found between subscales for emotional sensitivity, sympathy or distance.

The Interpersonal Reactivity Index (IRI; Davis, 1980, 1983) defines empathy in the context of broader psychological processes for emotional control, with subscales measuring levels of empathic concern and personal distress, as well as cognitive perspective-taking and fantasy abilities. Negligibly small effect was found between empathic concern and personal distress in correlational analyses. Other scales did not show correlational evidence between (cognitive and fantasy) subscales or empathic accuracy.

The Index of Empathy for Children and Adolescents (Bryant, 1982) is a self-rated questionnaire, similar to Davis' IRI for a comprehensive dimensional analysis, as well as scores for older children on the basis of Mehrabian & Epstein's measures for levels of emotional reactivity. The Bryant empathy measure (BEMP; Bryant, 1982) is useful in estimating children's other-oriented attachment.

The Interpersonal Reactivity Index-short form (IRI-short form; Davis, 1980; Russell & Bryant, 2002), a 16-item short form, is measured along four scales to be entered in a step-wise regression model with the Bryant empathy total (BEMP) to estimate trait empathy as a dispositional measure for five constructs, consisting of self-attachment, other-attachment, self-other overlap for insecurity measures, and two scales measuring levels of prosocial principles and behavior tendencies as a function of cognitive perspective-taking abilities.

The Empathy Quotient (EQ; Baron-Cohen & Wheelwright, 2004) defines empathy as having a cognitive (motivational drive to recognizing others' mental states) and affective (appropriate affective response to others' mental states) components. The EQ is used to help explain individual differences in affective responding and emotional stability/balance. Limitations for affective empathy include definitive properties that fail to distinguish between affective empathy, sympathy, and personal distress as emotion reaction constructs.

The State-Trait Anxiety Inventory (STAI; Spielberger, Gorusch, & Lushene, 1964; Guillene-Riquelma & Buela-Casal, 2011) declares that situation-specific stress responses are distinguished from stable dispositions for the tendency to experience negative emotions. Recent analyses have led to the development of emotional reactivity measures as a function of anxiety-induced experiences. Attachment Style Questionnaire (Appendix A) is a measure of anxiety, to distinguish between attachment insecurities on the basis of anxiety or avoidance.

Research Question(s)

To what extent is anxiety related to the inability to show empathy toward others?

Hypothesis

H_0: There is no difference between individuals with anxiety and the ability to show empathy toward others.

$$\mu1=\mu2$$

$\mu1$=individuals with anxiety
$\mu2$=individuals who possess the ability to show empathy toward others

H_1: Anxiety is negatively correlated with the ability to show empathy toward others.

$$\mu1\neq\mu2$$

$\mu1$=securely attached individuals
$\mu2$=insecurely attached individuals

Variables

The independent variables in this study include:

IV: anxiety – defined as a constant state of physiological arousal triggered by stimuli evoking a nervous system response to perceived threat to the self or one's safety; anxiety is measured by skin conductance and elevated heart rate associated with a physiological state of arousal to perceived threat. Level of measurement will take place along a nominal scale as a categorical measure.

The dependent variables include:

DV: empathy – characterized by the two dimensions for empathic ability: the capacity for emotional concern and the ability for cognitive perspective-taking for objective points of view; both cognitive and emotional dimensions allow for understanding of another's psychological state, as well as their state of mind. Level of measurement will take place along an interval scale.

Chapter 4
Participants

The target population consists of 150 participants, comparing local samples of middle and high school students, as well as college undergraduates. Students are given credit for participation applied to their course grades. Students represent a diverse population ranging in ages from pre-adolescence to young adulthood, to measure across age, race, gender, and individual differences that may generate any other sources of variance in the datasets.

Design

Longitudinal secondary data and cross-sectional designs are utilized to maximize reliability and validity measures; social variability will show that insecure adolescents will likely focus their attention to internalized states, where a predisposition to experience negative emotions will cascade these subjects into emotional and cognitive rumination, limiting other-oriented perspective taking. Similarly, cultural variation should show that collectivistic cultures tend to focus on academic abilities or other variables which limit their scope of attention to affective expression and therefore they may display secure attachments with significant figures but otherwise fail in empathic abilities.

Materials

The Attachment Style Questionnaire (Appendix A) is used to measure levels of attachment security that are subjectively felt or perceived by participants. The 36-item test is arranged in a 7-point Likert-type scale to assess levels of self-reported anxiety and avoidance in close relationships with others. The test is designed to measure attachment style in terms of affective reactivity and emotional security; this information may be useful for explaining relationship patterns and dependency issues in relationships.

The Interpersonal Reactivity Index (Appendix B) is a 28-point self-rated index for examining participants' subjective thoughts and feelings in situation-specific scenarios. The 5-point descriptive scale is used to assess patterns for levels of emotional reactivity and cognitive awareness in the context of interpersonal relationships. Degree of self-reported emotional stability is measured across a variety of contexts. To further differentiate transient emotional states from enduring personality traits in behavioral measures, the *State Trait Anxiety Inventory* (Appendix C), a 20-item self-report questionnaire, is designed to measure anxiety in adolescents and adults, assesses emotional reactivity (*STAI*; Spielberger, Gorusch, & Lushene, 1964). Validated for its psychometric use as a valid tool for distinguishing interpersonal, situation-specific stress response as quantitatively discrete from dispositional qualities (Guillene-Riquelma & Buela-Casal, 2011), emotional reactivity is shown to derive from anxiety experiences. Situation-specific interpersonal factors therefore reactivate stress response patterns, to perceived threats against self-constructs as well as avoidance of their negative effects.

Hoffman's Empathy Scales for self-serving stories are used to measure levels of empathy by testing individual differences. The above-mentioned Interpersonal Reactivity Inventory (*IRI*; Davis, 1983) uses a multidimensional analysis to analyze the factors that contribute to empathy and explore the role of cognition in perspective-taking abilities. Hoffman (2000) describes social stories as situations which trigger our natural reactions to employing moral beliefs. Empathy as an emotional construct was measured originally in 1972 as an emotional scale (*QMEE*; Mehrabian & Epstein, 1972) and later revised to measure emotional balance (*BEES*; Mehrabian, 2000), which currently remains unpublished today. Another popular and more recent self-report questionnaire which considers empathy in both emotional and cognitive respects utilize the empathy quotient (EQ) to explain individual differences in affect as well as stability (*EQ SQ theory*; Baron-Cohen & Wheelwright, 2004).

Procedure

Participants will be asked to complete a test battery which looks at the effects of anxiety, gender, age, attachment style, and dimensions of prosocial behavior, including sympathy, to measure their relative effects on empathy and related behaviors. The series of self-report measures examines the quantitative aspects of emotional development through testing procedures which are given to adolescents as well as their caregivers (typically their parents). Self-report inventories are taken with other-rated behavioral measures to compare against measures which check for malingering and socially desirable responding. Participants are then analyzed for their affective and cognitive capabilities for exhibiting empathic behavior toward others.

Discussion

The results indicate that many correlations exist, measuring individual differences such as sympathy, prosocial behavior, gratitude, anxiety, and attachment security in order to determine the general trends in the data. Data describes patterns between the variables, accounting for attachment security to lead to healthy development and prosocial tendencies; in contrast, attachment insecurities lead to anxious or avoidant responding to helping those in need.

Summary

Due to the data, we can reject the null hypothesis, and conclude that there is a difference between those with anxiety and those that have the ability to display empathy to others. There are some instances, however, such as social anxiety for egoistic motivations, which may account for variance and thus lead to empathy ability, despite anxiety.

Chapter 5

References

Barr, J. J., & D'Alessandro, A. H. (2007). Adolescent empathy and prosocial behavior in the multidimensional context of school culture. *Journal of Genetic Psychology, 168*(3), 231-250.

Batson, C. D., Fultz, J., & Schoenrade, P. (1997). Distress and Empathy: Two Qualitatively Distinct Vicarious Emotions with Different Motivational Consequences. *Journal of Personality, 55,* 19-39.

Baumeister, R. F., Leary, M. R. (1995). The need to belong: Desire for interpersonal attachments as a fundamental human motivation. P*sychological Bulletin, 117,* 497-529.

Bowlby, J. (1982). *Attachment and loss: Vol. 1. Attachment* (2nd ed.). New York, NY: Basic Books.

Bryant. B. K. (1982). Index of empathy for children and adolescents. *Child Development, 53,* 413-425.

Cacioppo, J. T., & Sandman, C. A. (1978). Physiological differentiation of sensory and cognitive tasks as a function of warning processing demands and reported unpleasantness. *Biological Psychobiology, 6,* 181-192.

Cassidy, J., & Kobak, R. R. (1988). Avoidance and its relationship with other defensive processes. In J. Belsky & T. Nezworski (Eds.), *Clinical implications of attachment* (pp. 300-323). Hillsdale, NJ: Erlbaum.

Culotta, C. M., & Goldstein, S. E. (2008). Adolescents' aggressive and prosocial behavior: Associations with jealousy and social anxiety. *Journal of Genetic Psychology, 169*(1), 21-33.

Davis, M. A. (1980). Multidimensional approach to individual differences in empathy. *JSAS Catalog of Selected Documents in Psychology, 10,* 85.

Eisenberg, N. (2000). Empathy and Sympathy. Ed. M. Lewis and J. M. Haviland-Jones, *Handbook of Emotions,* 677-691. New York/London: Guilford Press.

Eisenberg, N. (2009). Empathy-related responding: Links with self-regulation, moral judgment, and moral behavior. In M. Mikulincer & P. Shaver (Eds*.), Prosocial motives, emotions, and behavior.* Washington, DC: APA Publications.

Eisenberg, N., Fabes, R. A., Bustamante, D., Mathy, R. M., Miller, P., & Lindholm, E. (1988). Differentiation of vicariously induced emotional reactions in children. *Developmental Psychobiology, 24*, 237-246.

Eisenberg, N., Schaller, M., Fabes, R. A., Bustamante, D., Mathy, R., Shell, R., & Rhodes, K. (1988). The differentiation of personal distress and sympathy in children and adults. *Developmental Psychobiology, 24*, 766-775.

Fujisawa, K. K., Kutsukake, N., & Hasegawa, T. (2008). Reciprocity of prosocial behavior in Japanese preschool children. *International Journal of Behavioral Development, 32*(2), 89-97.

Frankfort-Nachmias, C., & Nachmias, D. (2008). *Research methods in the social sciences* (7th ed.). New York, NY: Worth Publishers.

Hein, G., & Singer, T. (2010). Neuroscience meets social psychology: An integrative approach to human empathy and prosocial behavior: The better angels of our nature (pp. 109-125). In M. Mikulincer & P. R. Shaver (Eds.), *Prosocial motives, emotions, and behavior.* Washington, DC: American Psychological Association.

Hoffman, M. (2000). *Empathy and Moral Development,* Cambridge: Cambridge University Press.

Krishnan, V., & Nestler, E. (2008). The molecular neurobiology of depression. *Nature, 455*(7215), 894-902.

Lang, S., Yu, T., Markl, A., Muller, F., & Kotchoubey, B. (2011). Hearing others' pain: Neural activity related to empathy. *Cognitive, Affective & Behavioral Neuroscience, 11*(3), 386-395.

Malti, T., Gummerum, M., & Buchmann, M. (2009). Children's moral motivation, sympathy, and prosocial behavior. *Child Development, 80*(2), 442-460.

Marteau, M., & Bekker, H. (1992). The development of a six-item short-form of the state scale of the Spielberger State-Trait Anxiety Inventory (STAI). *British Journal of Clinical Psychology* (1992), **31**, 301-306.

Mehrabian, A., & Epstein, N. (1972). A Measure of Emotional Empathy. *Journal of Personality, 40*, 525-543.

Mikulincer, M., & Shaver, P. R. (2007). *Attachment in adulthood: Structure, dynamics, and change.* New York, NY: Guilford Press.

Mikulincer, M., Shaver, P. R., & Rom, E. (2011). The effects of implicit and explicit security priming on creative problem solving. *Cognition and Emotion, 25*(3), 519-531. doi:10.1080/02699931.2010.540110

Mooradian, T. A., Davis, M., & Matzler, K. (2011). Dispositional empathy and the hierarchical structure of personality. *The American Journal of Psychology, 124*(1), 99-102.

Pelligra, V. (2011). Empathy, guilt-aversion, and patterns of reciprocity. *Journal of Neuroscience, Psychology, and Economics, 4*(3), 161-173. doi:10.1037/a0024688

Preston, S. D., & de Waal, F. B. (2002). Empathy: Its ultimate and proximate bases. *Behavioral and Brain Sciences, 25,* 1-20.

Russell, R. L., & Bryant, F. (2002). Purifying dispositional empathy: An interpersonal reactivity index short form. Paper presented at the American Psychological Association, Chicago, IL, August.

Shaver, P. R., & Mikulincer, M. (2012). An attachment perspective on morality: Strengthening authentic forms of moral decision making. In M. Mikulincer, P. R. Shaver (Eds.), *The social psychology of morality: Exploring the causes of good and evil* (pp. 257-274). Washington, DC US: American Psychological Association.

Scheler, M. (1973). *Wesen und Form der Sympathie.* Bern/Munchen, Francke Verlag (Engl. 1974) Translation: *The Nature of Sympathy,* London: Routledge & Kegan Paul.

Spielberger, C. D. (1983). Manual for the State-Trait Anxiety Inventory STAI (Form Y). Palo Alto, CA: Consulting Psychologists Press.

Snowden, J. (2003). *Empathy Predicts Relationship Constructs: Attachment, Self—Other Overlap, and Prosocial Orientation.* Washington, District of Columbia, US: American Psychological Association.

Thompson, R. A. (2010). Feeling and understanding through the prism of relationships. In S. D. Calkins, M. Bell (Eds.), *Child development at the intersection of emotion and recognition* (pp. 79-95). American Psychological Association. doi:10.1037/12059-005

APPENDICES

A. ATTACHMENT STYLE

http:www.web-research-design.net/cgi-bin/crq.pl

The Statements below concern how you feel in emotionally intimate relationships. We are interested in how you *generally* experience relationships, not just in what is happening in a current relationship. Respond to each statement by clicking a circle to indicate how much you agree or disagree with the statement. When you have answered all the questions, the web page will determine your *attachment style*.

_____ Top of Form _____

1. I worry that I won't measure up to other people.
   Strongly Disagree Strongly Agree

2. I find it easy to depend on romantic partners.
   Strongly Disagree Strongly Agree

3. When my partner is out of sight, I worry that he or she might become interested in someone else.
   Strongly Disagree Strongly Agree

4. When I show my feelings for romantic partners, I'm afraid they will not feel the same about me.
   Strongly Disagree Strongly Agree

5. It makes me mad that I don't get the affection and support I need from my partner.
   Strongly Disagree Strongly Agree

6. It's not difficult for me to get close to my partner.
   Strongly Disagree Strongly Agree

7. I am nervous when partners get too close to me.
   Strongly Disagree Strongly Agree

8. My partner really understands me and my needs.
   Strongly Disagree Strongly Agree

9. I don't feel comfortable opening up to romantic partners.
   Strongly Disagree Strongly Agree

10. I find that my partner(s) don't want to get as close as I would like.
    Strongly Disagree Strongly Agree

11. I talk things over with my partner.
    Strongly Disagree Strongly Agree

12. I often worry that my partner doesn't really love me.
    Strongly Disagree Strongly Agree

13. I often wish that my partner's feelings for me were as strong as my feelings for him or her.
    Strongly Disagree Strongly Agree

14. It's easy for me to be affectionate with my partner.
    Strongly Disagree Strongly Agree

15. I often worry that my partner will not want to stay with me.
    Strongly Disagree Strongly Agree

16. I am very comfortable being close to romantic partners.
    Strongly Disagree Strongly Agree

17. I'm afraid that I will lose my partner's love.
    Strongly Disagree Strongly Agree

18. I do not often worry about being abandoned.
    Strongly Disagree Strongly Agree

19. I find it relatively easy to get close to my partner.
    Strongly Disagree Strongly Agree

20. My romantic partner makes me doubt myself.
    Strongly Disagree Strongly Agree

21. When my partner needs some space, I don't take it personally.
    Strongly Disagree Strongly Agree

22. It is hard to express my feelings to my partner.
    Strongly Disagree Strongly Agree

23. My partner makes me feel better about my shortcomings.
    Strongly Disagree Strongly Agree

24. It is important for me to have my space in romantic relationships.
    Strongly Disagree Strongly Agree

25. When I break up with a romantic partner, it usually only takes me a couple days to get over him or her.
    Strongly Disagree Strongly Agree

26. I am more comfortable discussing my problems and concerns with friends than my partner.
    Strongly Disagree Strongly Agree

27. I hide a lot of things from my partner.
    Strongly Disagree Strongly Agree

28. My private thoughts are really none of my partner's business.
    Strongly Disagree Strongly Agree

29. I don't like to depend on romantic partners for anything.
    Strongly Disagree Strongly Agree

30. I try to be around my partner as much as I can.
    Strongly Disagree Strongly Agree

31. It is very important for me to have some 'alone time' away from my partner.
    Strongly Disagree Strongly Agree

32. I often find myself wondering what my partner thinks about me.
   Strongly Disagree Strongly Agree

33. Romantic partners usually seem to have stronger feelings for me than I do for them.
   Strongly Disagree Strongly Agree

34. I am so used to doing things on my own that I don't ask my partner for help.
   Strongly Disagree Strongly Agree

35. I am comfortable relying on my partner in times of need.
   Strongly Disagree Strongly Agree

36. I enjoy engaging in public displays of affection.
   Strongly Disagree Strongly Agree

B. INTERPERSONAL REACTIVITY INDEX

http://etd.ohiolink.edu/send-pdf.cgi/Capuano%20Angela%20M.pdf?bgsu1180535095

The following statements inquire about your thoughts and feelings in a variety of situations. For each item, indicate how well it describes you by choosing the appropriate letter on the scale at the top of the page: A, B, C, D, or E. When you have decided on your answer, fill in the letter in the appropriate column. READ EACH ITEM CAREFULLY BEFORE RESPONDING. Answer as honestly as you can. Thank you.

ANSWER SCALE:
A B C D E
DOES NOT DESCRIBE ME – DESCRIBES ME VERY WELL
Question Answer
(A, B, C, D, E)

1. I daydream and fantasize, with some regularity, about things that might happen to me.
2. I often have tender, concerned feelings for people less fortunate than me.
3. I sometimes find it difficult to see things from the "other guy's" point of view.
4. Sometimes I don't feel very sorry for other people when they are having problems.
5. I really get involved with the feelings of the characters in a novel.
6. In emergency situations, I feel apprehensive and ill-at-ease.
7. I am usually objective when I watch a movie or play, and I don't often get completely caught up in it.
8. I try to look at everybody's side of a disagreement before I make a decision.
9. When I see someone being taken advantage of, I feel kind of protective towards them.
10. I sometimes feel helpless when I am in the middle of a very emotional situation.
11. I sometimes try to understand my friends better by imagining how things look from their perspective.
12. Becoming extremely involved in a good book or movie is somewhat rare for me.
13. When I see someone get hurt, I tend to remain calm.
14. Other people's misfortunes do not usually disturb me a great deal.
15. If I'm sure I'm right about something, I don't waste much time listening to other people's arguments.
16. After seeing a play or movie, I have felt as though I were one of the characters
17. Being in a tense emotional situation scares me.
18. When I see someone being treated unfairly, I sometimes don't feel very much pity for them.
19. I am usually pretty effective in dealing with emergencies.

20. I am often quite touched by things that I see happen.
21. I believe that there are two sides to every question and try to look at them both.
22. I would describe myself as a pretty soft-hearted person.
23. When I watch a good movie, I can very easily put myself in the place of a leading character.
24. . I tend to lose control during emergencies.
25. When I'm upset at someone, I usually try to "put myself in his shoes" for a while.
26. When I am reading an interesting story or novel, I imagine how I would feel if the events in the story were happening to me.
27. When I see someone who badly needs help in an emergency, I go to pieces.
28. Before criticizing somebody, I try to imagine how I would feel if I were in their place.

Self-Report Measures for Love and Compassion Research: Empathy *NOTE: (-) denotes item to be scored in reverse fashion PT = perspective-taking scale FS = fantasy scale EC = empathic concern scale PD = personal distress scale A = 0 B = 1 C = 2 D = 3 E = 4 Except for reversed-scored items, which are scored: A = 4 B = 3 C = 2 D = 1 E = 0

C. STATE-TRAIT ANXIETY INVENTORY
Example from the Self-Evaluation Questionnaire (STAI-AD)

The development of a six-item short-form of the state scale of the Spielberger State-Trait Anxiety Inventory (STAI), wherein a number of statements which people have used to describe themselves, are given. Select the appropriate button to indicate how you feel *right now*; that is, at *this moment*. There are no right or wrong answers. Do not spend too much time on any one statement, but give the answer which seems to describe your present feelings best.

(Example:)

1. I feel upset.

         1   2   3   4
    (Not at all) – (Somewhat) – (Moderately so) – (Very much so)
2. I feel at ease
3. I feel upset
4. I am presently worrying over possible misfortunes
5. I feel satisfied
6. I feel uncomfortable
7. I feel self-confident
8. I feel nervous
9. ....
    ...(etc.).

---

*sample items are not authorized for reuse or modification; disclosing more than we have authorized will compromise the integrity and value of the instrument.

Theresa M. Marteau* and Hilary Bekker Health Psychology Unit, Royal Free Hospital School of Medicine, London NW3 2QG, UK

Anxiety and Depression Subscales: A Correlational Analysis

Amy Twilegar
November 18, 2014

Abstract

In the following set of studies, twenty ($n=20$) adult participants were given self-report surveys measuring rates of anxiety and depression, compared within individual assessments as well as between nominal groups. It is hypothesized that higher rates of anxiety should be positively correlated with higher rates for depression; upon further examination, it was determined that qualitatively common patterns emerged between variables for within-individual responses; in particular, those who claimed to have anxiety in general tended to respond similarly across scores measuring situation-specific variables and thus fostered further interest in comparative views. Overall, the data suggests a high level of correlation between anxiety and depression rates, suggesting the trait-based categories to be linked as comorbid events. Participants that showed higher levels of depression as having corresponding rates of anxiety were shown to foster a linear relationship positively connecting the two constructs. Further meta-analyses showed similar trends, as will be discussed in greater detail, to supplement these views.

In the following set of studies, the prevalence of anxiety-related tendencies was measured against rates of depression, all with whom test subjects were evaluated in prior surveys to fit particular groups concerning attentional dissent. All participants were instructed to privately fill out a set of surveys measuring levels of anxiety and depression across different contexts and settings, as self-report rates of symptom experiences and expressions for both constructs. The hypothesis posits individuals that experience frequent and consistent rates of subjective states for each category would show similarity within specified variables of each subjective state across contexts for self- and socially-mediated arousal states, as well as levels (self-rated frequencies of experience) for generalized categorical terms based on current nomenclature, and that these groups of individuals would show a positive linear relationship between groups, overall.

Methods

Twenty (*n* = 20) adult participants were measured for self-report questionnaire responses to a nominal set of qualities related to anxiety and depression (See Appendix A). A set of two surveys were given to each, to respond in yes/no answers, as well as measures for Introversion vs. Extraversion across a total of 25 and 28 questions, respectively. With demographic variables controlled for, subjects were presented with generalized subscales that correspondingly measured responses in accordance with anxiety and depression scales with respect to construct criteria. Measures were then calculated across variables, in addition to cross-group references to measure relationships between categorical data sets to further examine the relationship between the two specified groups.

Quantified measures for within-subject reliability between specified answers relating to anxiety across different variables were assessed. Consistency across homogenous answers regarding self-perceived levels of symptoms and social tendencies for generalized anxiety states, symptom severity in isolation settings and patterned behaviors, were observed. In the Depression questionnaire, data was compared for within-subject report measures across variables for experienced symptom levels for depressive episodes, as well as their relationships to anxious states. A second set of data measures were then analyzed to reveal patterns between those claiming to have anxiety as a generalized state of arousal experienced against that of depressive rates, and compared with self-perceived anxious tendencies to that of generally experienced frequent depressive states.

A value of +1 was assigned to those responses eliciting a "yes" response to questions, and a value of -1 to those responses for "no" to each individual score. The individual responses to questions whose "yes/no" replies were interpreted as ambiguous thus received a zero (0) value for these measures and were considered negligible for scoring purposes.

Results

The data suggests individuals with anxiety-related experiences whose scores were higher for generalized feelings of anxiety experienced similar feelings of anxiety in social conditions; in addition, these individuals tended to have higher rates of responses relative to that of symptom severity, and had more frequent occurrences of feeling anxious in general. Similarly, these response rates showed consistency in behavioral patterns specific to that of depressive feelings following anxiety-driven states. Responses to rates for depression were also shown to reveal a consistent pattern of data, measuring the relative rates of depression experienced across symptom prevalence, as well as feelings of depression as they strongly correlated with feelings of anxious tendencies in a similar manner. Measures were then compared between groups for anxiety and depression, based on percentage (%) levels of prevalence for each category, showing a strong positive relationship between higher rates of anxiety to be significantly correlated with rates of depression, in general. The findings show a strong positive co-relationship between individual variables as well as across anxiety and depression groups (See Data figures). No correlations were found between anxiety and depression subscales relative to Extroversion and Introversion trait measures and thus were considered negligible confines unnecessary for further review.

Percentage for Responses for Anxiety and Depression Subscales

	# Questions	24	28	

Individual	Anxiety +	Anxiety -	Depression +	Depression -	Anxiety +
1	8	16	11	13	33.33%
2	13	11	19	5	54.17%
3	15	9	16	9	62.50%
4	3	18	6	18	12.50%
5	15	6	17	7	62.50%
6	15	9	13	11	62.50%
7	11	13	18	6	45.83%
8	20	3	18	5	83.33%
9	15	9	15	7	62.50%
10	16	5	18	6	66.67%
11	6	15	13	11	25.00%
12	6	14	6	17	25.00%
13	19	3	5	16	79.17%
14	10	13	4	20	41.67%
15	11	11	18	4	45.83%
16	12	8	13	11	50.00%
17	5	18	10	13	20.83%
18	16	7	22	2	66.67%
19	2	18	9	15	8.33%
20	6	17	11	12	25.00%

Depression +	Anxiety -	Depression -	Anxiety	Depression
39.29%	66.67%	46.43%	-33.33%	-7.14%
67.86%	45.83%	17.86%	8.33%	50.00%
57.14%	37.50%	32.14%	25.00%	25.00%
21.43%	75.00%	64.29%	-62.50%	-42.86%
60.71%	25.00%	25.00%	37.50%	35.71%
46.43%	37.50%	39.29%	25.00%	7.14%
64.29%	54.17%	21.43%	-8.33%	42.86%
64.29%	12.50%	17.86%	70.83%	46.43%
53.57%	37.50%	25.00%	25.00%	28.57%
64.29%	20.83%	21.43%	45.83%	42.86%
46.43%	62.50%	39.29%	-37.50%	7.14%
21.43%	58.33%	60.71%	-33.33%	-39.29%
17.86%	12.50%	57.14%	66.67%	-39.29%
14.29%	54.17%	71.43%	-12.50%	-57.14%
64.29%	45.83%	14.29%	0.00%	50.00%
46.43%	33.33%	39.29%	16.67%	7.14%
35.71%	75.00%	46.43%	-54.17%	-10.71%
78.57%	29.17%	7.14%	37.50%	71.43%
32.14%	75.00%	53.57%	-66.67%	-21.43%
39.29%	70.83%	42.86%	-45.83%	-3.57%

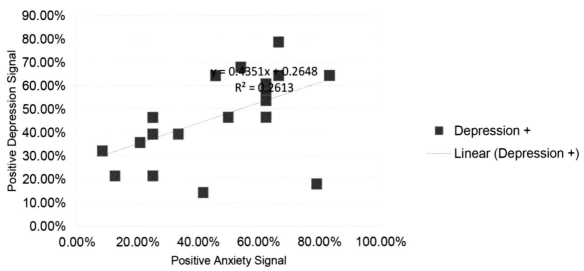

Positive Anxiety vs. Depression Signals

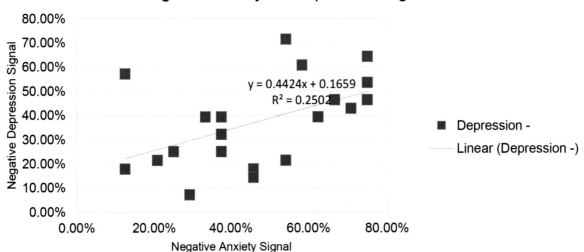

Negative Anxiety vs. Depression Signals

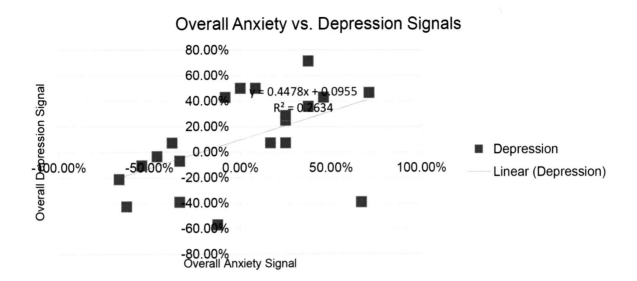

Overall Anxiety vs. Depression Signals

$y = 0.4478x + 0.0955$
$R^2 = 0.2634$

- Depression
- Linear (Depression)

Overall Depression Signal

Overall Anxiety Signal

Discussion

The data shows consistency between participants showing higher rates of anxiety symptoms compared to those experiencing depressive states. The underlying nature of these integral relationships shows a generalized pattern of correlational trends, suggesting a relative anxious disposition mediates that of depressive states. The rates of responses to the two subscales of behavior implies a co-linear relationship between opposing physiological patterns to be inextricably intertwined. This suggests a spectral-like quality between hyper-active and hypo-active nervous system arousal patterns may be intrinsically interlinked. The role of these activation patterns in their shared prominence when examining mental disorders such as ADHD are further examined in greater detail to conjugate these trends.

Would you consider yourself to be "anxious?" _____

("anxious" as defined by general feelings of nervousness, across contexts and various conditions)

Do you consider yourself to have test anxiety? _____

Do you often feel social pressure elicits behaviors you normally wouldn't perform? _____

Do you often find yourself fidgeting, or otherwise exhibiting stereotypies? _____

("stereotypies"' as defined by repetitive movements such as twirling your hair or tapping feet)

Are you nervous before giving public speeches, regardless of the crowd? _____

Do you find yourself worrying about what others think a majority of the time? _____

Are you nervous in social situations among unfamiliar peers? _____

Do you find that you are restless, even when you are alone? _____

Would you consider yourself to be extraverted or introverted a majority of the time? _____

("extroverted" meaning gregarious and outgoing, "introverted" indicating social withdrawal)

Would you consider your comfort level to generally be mostly when you are alone?_____

Do you find yourself to be self-doubting when pressure to perform tasks arises? _____

in general, do you consider yourself to be insecure? _____

Have you ever been consistently "bullied" during any one phase of your life? _____

Do you consider yourself to be self-doubting when are expected to do well? _____

Has anyone ever told you that you are simply not good enough? _____

Do you experience anxiety when socially rejected or criticized in groups? _____

When you experience anxiety, do you ruminate on feeling this way? _____

In the presence of other people, do you find you compare yourself by default? _____

Do you find yourself staying active when feeling depressed or down? _____

Do you consider yourself "comfortable in your own skin" most of the time? _____

("comfortable in your own skin" to be indicative of your niche/environment)

Do you have more anxiety while test-taking, compared with social situations? _____

Do you find it hard to relax, even when you are alone? _____

Do you feel accepted in general, across social and family contexts? _____

Do you feel that others judge you, whether real or imagined? _____

———•◆•———

Do you often feel like you have nothing to contribute to society? _____

Are you often sad or depressed when reflecting on your life? _____

Would you consider yourself unworthy of achieving great things in your life? _____

Would you consider yourself as contributing to making changes in this world? _____

Do you ever feel anhedonia, or inability to find pleasure in everyday activities? _____

Do you generally experience sadness, or lack of pleasure in social events? _____

Are you generally satisfied with your life? _____

When you experience negative emotions, do you generally withdraw? _____

Do you feel you have the ability to self-regulate emotional states? _____

Have you ever had suicidal thoughts or harming oneself?_____

Do you ever feel that your self-worth is lower than others such as your peers? _____

Do you ever find at times that it is difficult to be productive for prolonged periods of time? _____

Do you often find yourself rejecting invitations to social events? _____

When experiencing negative emotions, do you find that this follows anxious episodes? _____

Are your parental or primary caregiver relationships "secure"? _____

    ("secure" meaning attachment security in safety and trust)

Do you often feel neglected when expressing your needs? _____

Do you often feel your life achievements are often overlooked? _____

Are your relationships with others generally supportive to your desires? _____

Do you have a sense of fulfillment when accomplishing achievements?_____

Do you generally feel tired with no apparent reasons why? _____

Are your day-to-day activities seemingly dull for multiple days at a time? _____

Do you sometimes feel sluggish or exhausted when well-rested and alert? _____

When experiencing depressed symptoms, do you feel relationships may counter these feelings? _____

Do you feel the need to turn to others when experiencing hardships in your life? _____

Do you find there are changes in your appetite when experiencing negative events? _____

Do you find that anxious tendencies are often correlated with depressive states? _____

Do you feel a sense of hopelessness when experiencing negative states? _____

When negativity in life arises, do you tend to experience changes in sleep patterns? _____

IV. The Biological Bases of ADHD

Amy M. Twilegar
Submission of Masters Thesis, M.A.
University of the Rockies, 2013

I. **Discuss the biological basis of ADHD. Identify any brain structures and neurotransmitters implicated in the etiology of this disorder.**

Attention Deficit Hyperactivity Disorder (ADHD) is classified as a behavioral disorder, characterized by inattention to salient cues in the environmental context, inability to sustain selective attention to target cues, and in some cases a hyperactive state which constitutes a behavioral disinhibition tendency and may be expressed as restlessness to the observer. Recent evidence to classify ADHD and its relative subcategories has shed light on the behavioral manifestations of ADHD as resulting from an insufficient neural networking mechanism stretching the frontal striatal cerebellar network in the brain, occupying the right hemispheric domain which shows a lack of oxygen metabolism across these areas when observing fMRI scans.

The Diagnostic and Statistical Manual of Mental Disorders currently considers personality disorders to be categorical syndromes that deviate from normal personality (DSM-IV-TR; American Psychological Association, 2000). Given the complexity of the disorder, ADHD research shows an alternative dimensional viewpoint reconsidering the rigidity underlying this distinction. Samuel and colleagues (2010) support this dimensional view, postulating personality pathology to be maladaptive, extreme expressions of general personality traits; researchers consider these extremities to exist at the latent level, expressions emerging at later stages in maladaptive ways. More recently, changes to these descriptions have included a greater focus on functional impairments, rather than structural properties (Skodol et al., 2011). Due to functional magnetic resonance imaging techniques, researchers can now identify the metabolic pathways interrupted by pervasive symptoms of ADHD.

Research shows the attentional networks in the brain as a shared neurobiological connection between the prefrontal cortex and limbic regions, suggesting the limited capacity to process information in a high arousal state may impede cognitive functioning such as thought organization and reasoning abilities. The hyperactive behavior characteristic of ADHD thus relates the dysfunction to a hyperarousal state. This biological setback is evident in those afflicted by the disorder, diminishing the capacity to sustain attention and may even interfere with memory encoding as well as retrieval. High stress conditions warrant the need to activate dopaminergic effects for fight-or-flight response to such events; having prolonged exposure to stress through the early, critical years thus justifies the argument that ADHD may be a product of early environment adjustments that predispose these cognitive defects.

II. Discuss the major psychopharmacological interventions for this disorder, the biological explanation of why this intervention is effective, and whether or not the research is conclusive.

Currently, there is controversy surrounding the idea of pharmacological drug treatment in comparison with therapeutic techniques to alleviate symptoms of ADHD, as well as comorbid conditions such as anxiety and depression. There exists today in research a translational gap in literature, describing the disparity that remains between disciplines for psychiatry and psychology. The biological emphasis of ADHD in adulthood raises many concerns in this regard, as clinical diagnostic criteria may create a barrier to functional behaviors that are observed. The psychiatric literature is founded on biological constraints to mentally ill patients, whereas case history studies in psychology outline the theoretical nature of the disease.

References

Samuel, D. B., Simms, L. J., Clark, L. A., Levesly, W. J., & Widiger, T. A. (2010). An item response theory

integration of normal and abnormal personality scales. *Personality Disorders: 1*(1), 5-21.

Samuel, D. B., Simms, L. J., Clark, L. A., Levesly, W. J., & Widiger, T. A. (2010). "An item response theory

integration of normal and abnormal personality scales": Correction to Samuel et al (2010). *Personality Disorders: Theory, Research, and Treatment, 1*(3), 191. doi: 10.1037/a0020496

Skodol, A. E., Clark, L., Bender, D. S., Krueger, R. F., Morey, L. C., Verheul, R., &...Oldham, J. M. (2011). Proposed changes in personality and personality disorder assessment and diagnosis for DSM-5

Part 1: Description and rationale. *Personality Disorders: Theory, Research, and Treatment, 2*(1), 4-22. doi: 10.1037/a0021891

V. The Role of Early Experiences in Shaping the Onset for ADHD in Adulthood

The role of early childhood experiences as a prospective risk factor for developing late onset symptoms of ADHD may intrinsically be construed as a challenge in explaining potential proneness for vulnerability to the development of the disorder having a latent trait expression quality as a result of maltreatment variables; however, there is sufficient evidence to conclude that latent trait expressions for risk factors such as the personality trait neuroticism, coupled with anxiety-driven constructs, as well as fear-based automation for nervous system reactivity to childhood maltreatment, may play key roles in the development of ADHD in adulthood. Childhood abuse, though loosely defined, can be a risk factor in and of itself; the predisposition of childhood maltreatment in the forms of neglect and/or abuse may be easier conceptualized when breaking symptomologies down to the biological level. The sympathetic nervous system reactivity patterns experienced through stress in early relationships, akin to fearful or abusive circumstances, may thereby become a catalyst for further developmental effects. Such effects may be hypervigilance, or overactive nervous system arousal states, having sustained and prolonged exposure to parental maltreatment contexts, forming patterned ways of adapting to abusive environments in the early years. These hypervigilant patterns, as a way to constantly be 'aware' of one's surroundings, such as in fear-based environments, may "program" the developing brain to constantly be "on-alert" to perceived threat exposure. Coupled with a sense of learned helplessness as a dependent child, in addition to a relentless fearful disposition, this may help to explain anxiety-related mechanisms as predisposed constructs associated with attentional disorders. This comorbid structure in personality pathology and developmental influence may then render utility in considering dispositional anomalies as maladaptive trends; in turn, this may set the stage for vulnerability to the acquisition of latent stage development for attentional difficulties seen in adult ADHD.

Several studies are recently emerging that not only qualitatively describe these vulnerabilities as high-risk factors for attentional consequences, but also point to the neurobiological constraints these experiences may impose to brain maturation processes, should the events ensue. The emergence of fMRI brain scans in comparing metabolic pathways interceded by inattention to salient cues is a laboratory-driven mechanism by which to grasp the calamity of neural network deficits across frontal-striatal-cerebellar networks in the brain in response to stress-induced events. This quantitative measurement serves to supplement the notion that across anxiety-related disorders, activation patterns show little change. The concept of childhood abuse as a precursor to anxiety-driven variables that can set the stage for later developmental detriments to the maturing brain is only at the forefront of conceptualizing the quality of upbringing as a necessary factor in diagnosing adult ADHD. Currently, the DSM-5 (American Psychiatric Association, 2013) states that adult onset for ADHD diagnoses has now widely been accepted; however, the idea that developmental factors such as childhood maltreatment variables is yet to exist as a factor for criteria in adults whose symptoms began in their early adulthood years.

Anxiety has been shown to contribute to, but not cause, the later development for this disorder; however, it is important to note that later onset development for this afflicting disease may be predisposed to the individual growing up in fear. Insecure attachments to parental figures in early relationships may present a clearer picture as to the detrimental effects. Neglectful relationships harboring uncaring or abandoning parental caregiver figures elicits a sense of mistrust. The fear of abandonment as a counter-product harbors maladaptive coping mechanisms, as the vulnerable child learns they may not count on their parents' return or meet their needs for comfort when that person leaves their sight; another facet to considering insecure attachment, typically within the primary caregiver relationship in the early years, is the absence of feeling safe. Safety, as defined by developmental researchers, constitutes the feeling of relational stability, thus feeling safe in knowing there is no need to worry or feel anxious, and that they are safe in a stable relationship with the person caring for them who won't simply just leave, or abandon, them in a general sense. According to John Bowlby (1969), a "feeling of being loved and a sense of belonging is one of the most basic human needs." This is highly jeopardized with regard to attachment when considering the detrimental effects on the developing brain when early attachment relationships are devoid of such necessities, and thus result in negative effects.

Research on early attachment relationships and their impacts on social behavior reveals childhood stress to be a potential correlate in delayed brain maturation processes for maladjusted trends; findings reveal this to possibly constitute a risk factor in correlating with the development for ADHD (Grossman & Avital, 2023). Developmental milestones are gained with each critical phase of learning; throughout childhood, adolescence and young adulthood, learning to cope with and adapt to environmental challenges sets the stage for differential achievements progressive throughout each successive stage. In childhood, typically one learns attachment security (or insecurities, depending on the nature of relationship between primary caregiver and child); children also learn rules and obedience, and that they can have a mind of their own. In adolescence, children typically learn to self-regulate their emotional states and patterns, and in young adulthood, individuals typically learn to think on their own; during this latter phase, the next set of close attachment relationships begin to emerge, that of which have strong influences from early attachment relationships formed in caretaker-child dyads, and these patterned behaviors in social contexts typically have long-standing consequential effects.

Research for data analysis from Census 2021 (Elkin, 2020) contends the difficulty in measuring the scale and nature of abusive relationships experienced in childhood, due to hidden factors and case history reports. Despite these limitations, documented reports for such occurrences have been found to provide substantial evidence supporting the argument that consequential effects of abuse in childhood show marked correlations to disabilities later seen in adults. Data show that adults who report having illness and daily functional impairments were significantly more likely to have suffered abuse prior to 16 years of age (see Fig. 5).

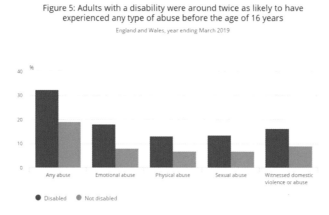

Figure 5: Adults with a disability were around twice as likely to have experienced any type of abuse before the age of 16 years
England and Wales, year ending March 2019

Supported by recent research, there are commonalities shared between adults and children in brain imaging scans to show observable alterations in neurobiological studies (Cupertino et al., 2020); however, according to researchers, though such overlaps can be seen between age-specific cohorts, a larger multivariate prediction model (Wolfers et al., 2019) was necessary for further review to determine etiological bases underlying such behaviors exhibited by test subjects. These pathophysiological features for outlining restrictive functioning lend insight to the utility in mapping theoretical constructs onto biological data such as observable evidence generated by fMRI scans; after controlling for demographic variables, it shows valid scientific evidence for such neurocognitive deficits to be present in ADHD subjects across age-related groups. Nevertheless, developmental milestones for learning patterned responses to maladaptive events, necessitates a closer look at early experiences to explain developmental effects.

Furthermore, abusive relationships experienced in the early years may also have cataclysmic adversities when trauma is factored in. Taken into account that fearful reactions are introduced, it seems the need to factor in the physiological consequences such as automated responses from trauma and the resultant negative effects. A hypervigilant child thus adapts to fearful conditions when parental abuse is introduced. Subsequently, the aforementioned aversive stimuli "primes" the brain to be hypervigilant in constant states of preparedness, to become simply an adaptive acquired ability with threat perception to the developing brain from which it learns. These qualities, as research has shown, tend to reduce in severity of symptoms in the adolescent years; however, the final critical phase of development for brain maturation processes regarding emotional self-regulation patterns and attentional capacities, may still be at risk for vulnerability to such injurious effects.

Resilience in the adolescent phase of development may prove to be fruitless when the early adulthood years renders insecure attachment in the next set of intimate relationships, critical for maturational processes in brain development for secure attachment bonds. Maladaptive patterns for emotional dysregulation strategies and resultant behavioral sequelae may therefore continue into later years, given the critical phase for learning and development within this maturational stage. Should the emerging adult (20—22 years, typically) experience relational instability once again, this may jeopardize their sense of perceived security in attachment relationships and re-kindle these harrowing fears. With a faulty sense of trust and uncertainty in relationships, the individual's prospects of finally finding themselves in a safe environment now mimics the former past; attention problems and prior obstacles in overcoming these challenging constructs likely will re-emerge. At the cost of attentional capacities, with only so much amount to allocate toward the delicate balance between prefrontal cortical regions and amygdala in the brain, the patterns of maladaptive responses to stressful situations and fearful reactions fall victim to maturational factors across regions for higher order cognitive functioning processes and emotion regulation to their demise. Thus, internalization processes for attentional capacities, directed to internal experiences inside, now focuses on the distress experienced within the individual as a result. Consequently, this consumes their attentional capacities, rather than focusing on external cues in the environmental context, salient for learning and personal growth.

Internal Working Models are formed through the early years, as conceptualized mental schema-based representations of the environments by which we learn. Primary caregiver relationships help shape the contexts of attachment securities, in addition to situation-specific behavior patterns by which to adapt. Specifically, abusive experiences may therefore predispose the constructs currently recognized as comorbid tendencies relative to that of ADHD. Developing young brains often find adaptive ways to cope with or avoid distress; however, children dependent on abusive caregivers may feel helpless to these

45

harmful home events. Fear-based anxiety states and hypervigilance effects often predispose long-term consequences such as anxious reactivity patterns formed through the early years. Although resilience may be a key moderator in overcoming the negative effects, parental maltreatment patterns yet prevail in predisposing young children to maladaptive coping trends. Those who nevertheless endure the injurious effects of parental abuse still may be resilient enough to overcome such harmful experiences; those who are fortunate enough in such cases, however, face a disadvantage in early adulthood, should this critical developmental milestone introduce these patterns which tragically re-emerge. Toxicity in relational contexts may therefore re-ignite fear-based patterns of reactivity and set the stage for attentional deficits, which may render lifelong effects.

Since there is only so much attention that can be allocated between the pre-frontal cortex, responsible for higher order cognitive functioning processes, and limbic systems for regulating emotion, attentional capacities are mediated by cognitive control. Internalization processes directing attention to emotional distress thus impedes cognitive functioning abilities for clarity of mind, thereby inhibiting attention to salient cues in the environmental context at the sake of emotional discord.

Coupled with the personality trait neuroticism, the tendency to cognitively ruminate and dwell on negative experiences and emotions, these comorbid tendencies developed from early abuse thus sheds light on the predispositioned factors which may, if not resolved within by the early adult years, have lifelong lasting consequences. Neuroticism coupled with inattention to salient cues in the environmental context in place of internalized distress, therefore offer greater insight to the mature brain retaining such deficits in attentional capabilities, limiting the ability to selectively attend to other stimuli in the face of distressful experiences, thus reducing such cognitive control.

These internalization tendencies, relative to emotional instability factors, serve to reduce cognitive control over selective attentional shifts. With regard to attachment insecurities, early environmental influences harboring adapted behavioral trends can breed disadvantageously learned reactivity patterns and behavioral response tendencies as a result of environmental influences from the past; consequently, these patterned responses may lead to developmental difficulties in sustained attentional control. These functional impairments may thereby affect cognitive structural properties which can heavily influence behavioral dispositions by fostering maladaptive coping mechanism strategies learned from early experiences and manifested in later years. These consequential anomalies may therefore predispose ADHD-like symptomatology expressions which can furthermore have long-lasting antecedent effects. Thus, adult onset of ADHD diagnoses illustrates the need to examine symptomologies in the context of precursor events. This facilitates the need for case history variables to be considered regarding childhood abuse factors, denoting the etiological significance in the development of ADHD in adulthood; these factors may be important to consider, beyond conceptualizing late onset of ADHD criteria measures as simply an insurgent disorder of the brain.

In critically re-evaluating childhood factors for emergent properties of ADHD, it becomes salient to consider the quality of upbringing as a cascade of developmental events for predisposing patterned stress responses to traumatic experiences, leading up to the maladjusted symptoms which may better explain the development of ADHD in adulthood. In examining fMRI brain scans and taking a survey of childhood events, the greater awareness to biological mechanisms relative to psychosocial factors provides increased conceptualization of ADHD rather as a possibly maladaptive set of patterned responses developed throughout the early years. Perhaps the rigid structure of criteria in diagnosing adult ADHD may one day include childhood maltreatment variables to account for the neurobiological constraints afflicted by those whose early childhood trauma helps to explain the biological bases of behavior surrounding ADHD in psychiatric settings. In doing so, neuroimaging data sets, such as those produced from fMRI scans, may help to explain the underlying attentional deficits as possible products of childhood maltreatment variables, thus fostering utility in exploring these ideas in further review.

VI. NEUROBIOLOGICAL CORRELATES: fMRI SCANS

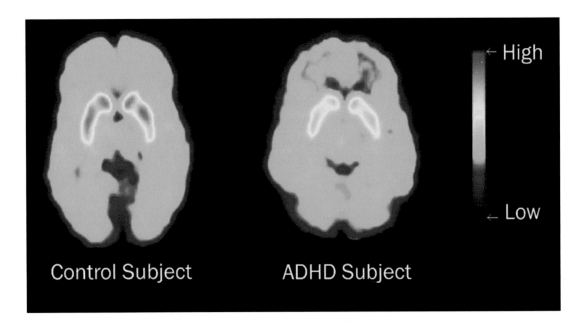

The fMRI scans for brain activity, shown above, reveals activation patterns dissimilar to that of controls, in metabolic pathways associated with ADHD. These highlighted regions reflect activity across specific brain regions which are observable patterns detected among corresponding patterns similar to that of PTSD, Bipolar Disorder, and Anxiety (Rosack, 2004).

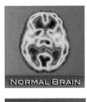

Although the distinctive brain regions associated with anxiety-related illnesses can be clearly observed in brain scans, it remains a mystery as to the etiology of this disease. It has been clearly shown that pharmacological intervention in the form of stimulant drugs can reduce emotional dysregulation and facilitate attention-driven networks to focus based on promoting higher-order cognitive functioning processes through greater attention control; brain mechanisms with greater capacity to selectively attend to external cues in the environmental context rather than internalized distress, show increased prefrontal activation patterns for greater attentional control. This cognitive deficit can be mediated by drug treatment, but the core issue remains as to etiological significance and how to incorporate these measures in controlled settings?

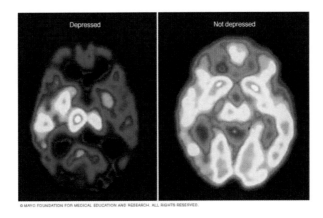

Accessed March 10, 2024, from: *https://www.treat-major-depression.com*
Mayo Clinic (2018). *PET scan of the brain for depression.* Available at: www.mayoclinic.org

Comparative evaluations cross-referencing differential brain systems in analyzing fMRI scans in individuals for such disorders currently known to represent the comorbid qualities associated with ADHD are reviewed at length. The cognitive faculties observed share a concrete set of appraisals when identifying distinctive brain functioning activation across hemispheric domains.

VII. STATISTICAL FINDINGS AMONG CONSTRUCTS

Childhood trauma (Edel, Weber, Brune, & Assion, in Press) examines the early effects of parental caregiving when discussing abusive relationships with early attachment figures and their relative effects on psychopathology in later years. Early traumatic influences were shown to affect not only children in emotion regulation processes, but share predominant patterns in traumatized adults with ADHD. The lingering effects of early trauma thus carry long-lasting effects across relationship contexts with attachment figures throughout the adulthood years.

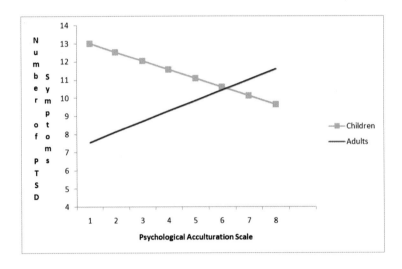

The consequence of recurrent emotional dysfunction in relationships due to abusive contexts, having experienced sustained trauma, highlights a pattern that re-emerges if not resolved within. This may afflict greater suffering, should this pattern re-emerge in later years. Maladaptive coping mechanisms account for the patterned effect, disrupting the victimized individual with future relationships and maladjustments to interpersonal conflicts and perceived stress.

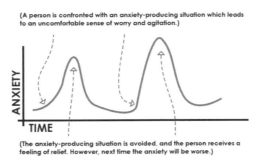

(A person is confronted with an anxiety-producing situation which leads to an uncomfortable sense of worry and agitation.)

(The anxiety-producing situation is avoided, and the person receives a feeling of relief. However, next time the anxiety will be worse.)

https://www.therapistaid.com/images/content/guide/cbt-for-anxiety/anxiety-time.png

The preconceived notion that perception affects attention holds critical value when considering trauma-related experiences and exposures to abusive childhood events. Feelings of fear, helplessness, uncertainty, and vulnerability all have negative consequential effects on the young, developing brain. Increased arousal in sympathetic nervous system activity, which leads to overactive brain systems for "fight or flight" mechanisms to be employed, may be correlated with an increased sense of 'edginess' and agitation; at the same time, these factors may also be expressed in terms of avoidance to reminders of the trauma experiences, and may manifest as things like irritability, hastiness to become angered, or even feelings of guilt or shame or dissociation to reality, such as social withdrawal. Hypervigilance, which may be associated with hyperactivity levels, fosters a heightened sense of awareness for perceived threats and may also constitute patterned response tendencies such as recklessness, aggressiveness, or even self-destructive behaviors.

The characteristic qualities for symptoms manifested in ADHD show similar overlap in constructs for distractibility, disorganization and restlessness; however, hyperactive behaviors tend to mimic the anxious patterns observed. Such symptoms appear to denote the impatience, fidgeting, squirming, and even trouble sleeping seen typically in ADHD patients. This hyperactive nervous system arousal is also shown to share similar patterns for those with anxiety, and furthermore shares similar activation patterns across conjunctive brain regions related to attention. The effects of early trauma can have detrimental effects on attention capabilities, all products of trauma experienced at an early age.

VIII. The Role of Parental Maltreatment in the Development of Adult ADHD

Studies have been conducted to explore the role of parental rearing behavior in relation to ADHD symptoms expressed in adulthood and resultant effects of early attachment relationships in symptom expression exhibited in later years (Edel, Edel, Kruger, Assion, Juckel, & Brune, 2015). Researchers examined emotion processing dysregulation, found to be a key symptom in those afflicted by ADHD, and its relative proclivity to early attachment relationships; it was found that dysfunctional patterns in emotion processing were mainly predicted by early or current attachment-related constructs, primarily in those suffering from ADHD. Thus, the quality of childhood rearing is shown to be a significant prognosticator for the development ADHD symptoms, seen in children as well as adults.

Taken together, the findings reveal the significance of early attachment relationships in the development of ADHD. Thus, it can be concluded that the quality of parental relationships formed in the early years may set the stage for emotional dysregulation patterns, thereby predisposing the risk for developing ADHD. These findings are very salient to understanding key risk factors for developing ADHD; however, these studies only reveal evidence of ADHD symptomatology across age groups, limiting a further consideration for examining the role of maltreatment variables to posing a risk factor for the development of ADHD in adulthood. Rather, it is simply concluded that dysregulated emotion patterns are present in children as well as adults.

A further study by Edel, Brune and Assion (in Press) more recently addresses the role of trauma experienced in early relationships to find that traumatized adults with ADHD highly corresponded to childhood trauma severity. These findings reveal childhood trauma to therefore be a significant predictor of ADHD observed in adults. Altogether, these studies show the role of childhood experiences in predicting ADHD in children as well as adults; this suggests the need to carefully re-examine risk factors such as comorbid traits, as well as developmental inferences, lending new insights to the etiological constructs and perspective approaches. Beyond the scope of observable risk factors, in turn, helps to elucidate developmental factors for emerging properties as well as precursor effects, to re-conceptualize the symptomatology variables for adult ADHD and thus view it in a constructively redefined way.

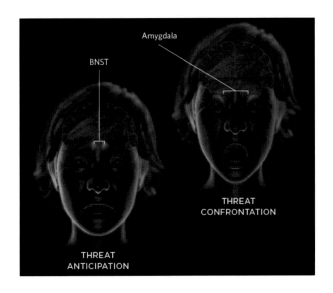

Amygdala

BNST

THREAT
CONFRONTATION

THREAT
ANTICIPATION

The purpose of introducing early year experiences in predisposing qualities which may render vulnerability to developing ADHD in adulthood must, in addition, be explored. The functional limitations imposed by childhood maltreatment may also be argued within the realm of resilience. This strengthened mental overture lends credence to being able as an individual to overcome traumatic experiences such as abusive environments; namely within the context of relational stability and emotional self-regulation patterning, this profound capability undermines the possibility of reversion during critical brain maturational phases for development in periods where further injury occurs. Although some may be fortunate in developing and sustaining resilience, having suffered from and overcoming early adverse effects from childhood events, re-occurrences such as feelings of abandonment and mistrust in stable relationships in later years can take a greater toll when brain maturational processes crystallize for emotional health. These cognitive deficits reflect a disordered psychological aptitude centered around dysregulation patterns re-activated in the face of insecurities surrounding attachment issues, with the results imposing devastation for maladjustments in dealing with these fears. Namely, the young adulthood years brings forth developmental milestones relative to that for largely determining lifelong trends. Thus, emotional regulation patterns within close, intimate relationships form patterned behavioral proclivities and likely remain dispositional tendencies that are shaped from early exposures to intimate relationships from the past. As such, these measures within context-driven behaviors elicits maturational brain mechanisms, foundationally casting the patterned behaviors for dispositional traits.

The resulting dysregulated patterns of emotional reactivity tendencies and behavioral response dispositions can thereby explicate these experiences for internalized feelings of distress as consuming cognitive capacity levels, and impede the functioning capabilities for selective attentional control. Feelings of anxiety, resulting from insecurely attached relationships, thereby set the stage for lifelong consequences of emotional discord in unstable relationships. These resultant negative affects thereby become patterns of responsivity measures to be more carefully considered when evaluating populations within the context of adult ADHD.

Research has shown that adversities in the relative domains in psychology during these critical phases for brain development in young adulthood years with whom acquire maladjustments in relationship contexts may retrospectively predict patterns of attentional dysregulation and control; as such, this may lead to dysregulated patterns for cognitive abilities to selectively control attentional shifts, thus inhibiting functional abilities for shifting attention to salient cues. Consequently, the internalization of the distress experienced within may likely foster lifelong struggling with ADHD-like symptoms, given during this time they are experienced again.

These findings are shown to be consistent among those self-perceived to experience patterned responses between these factors in evaluating feelings of attentional difficulties; although further research is necessary for identifying the intrinsic nature of these influences on the development of ADHD, it can be noted that the integral constructs have underlying comorbid symptomatology and should be factored in. The fundamental underpinnings for the propensity to acquire ADHD-like qualities should furthermore be considered to factor in the consequential facets of abusive and/or neglective childhood, adolescent and young adulthood experiences. The significant relationships between such variables thus shed greater insight to the developmental consequences and/or vulnerabilities to heighten the risk for behavioral and intrinsic anomalies in attentional networks in the brain, lending credence to the idea that maturation of brain anatomy as well as age-specific milestones and experiences in the early years may have detrimental effects on cognitive processing; namely, developmental implications for symptom expressions observed in adult-onset populations for ADHD. The evidence presented exemplifies the need to make provisions in re-considering the circumscribed variables that characteristically define the constructs for diagnosing adult ADHD.

IX.CLOSING THE TRANSLATIONAL GAP

The issue of adult ADHD is currently defined by a specified set of symptoms and it can be concluded that childhood upbringing has a significant impact on emotional states; this has shown to be a key risk factor in the advent of childhood maltreatment on emotional dysregulation patterns, as seen in adults. This holds important implications for clinical assessments in diagnosing adults with ADHD; however, the DSM-5 criteria remains critical in the diagnostic criteria requisites for adult ADHD diagnoses, retaining the assessment protocol within a confined set of measures.

The latest revision of DSM-5 has revised its set of criteria variables to expand its acceptance in diagnosing ADHD in adulthood; this holds great value in psychological practice for patients to receive adult diagnoses, and offers adults the advantage of being helped with their disability when ADHD is recognized, though often thought of and having been previously believed to be a childhood disorder. The specifications also give subtypes of categorical factors defining ADHD, from "inattentive" type as having an array of attentional limitations, to "hyperactive" as showing restlessness and impulsivity, among other variables, as well. These distinctions seem to follow a paradigm that mimics avoidance vs. anxious tendencies, that of which can be thought of conceptually as a fundamental comparison to depression vs. anxiety. Because these trait-based qualities are both seen at higher rates in individuals with ADHD, their comorbid qualities thus present a collaborative functional viewpoint in the direction for constructively re-labeling ADHD.

Anxiety, negatively correlated with empathy, is shown to positively correlate with depression, as well as positively correlating with hypervigilance, and further exacerbated with childhood maltreatment variables. Evidence suggests this variable may need to be contemplated slightly more when it comes to ADHD diagnoses. Presented below are the outlined criteria variables currently implemented in the classification and labeling of ADHD.

Avoidance and hyperactivity seem to divide the two categorical distinctions for ADD and ADHD based on hyperactivity which can otherwise be thought of as a by-product of hypervigilance. Interestingly, this hypervigilance, as shown to be a product of trauma experienced in childhood, has been shown in research to be interconnected to anxiety measures, and research has shown emotional dysregulation patterns to be evident with those who receive some form (or forms) of abuse in the early years. The concept of insecure attachment as described previously describes anxious/avoidance tendencies as forms of insecurity in relationships, that which stems from parental maltreatment experienced in early childhood relationships. Although traumatized adults have been shown to experience and exhibit ADHD-like symptoms across children and adults, as seen in the previous study, the implications thereby deductively link anxiety to ADHD.

DSM-5 Diagnostic Criteria for ADHD

	Symptoms and/or behaviors that have persisted ≥ 6 months in ≥ 2 settings (e.g., school, home, church). Symptoms have negatively impacted academic, social, and/or occupational functioning. In patients aged < 17 years, ≥ 6 symptoms are necessary; in those aged ≥ 17 years, ≥ 5 symptoms are necessary.
Inattentive Type Diagnosis Criteria	• Displays poor listening skills • Loses and/or misplaces items needed to complete activities or tasks • Sidetracked by external or unimportant stimuli • Forgets daily activities • Diminished attention span • Lacks ability to complete schoolwork and other assignments or to follow instructions • Avoids or is disinclined to begin homework or activities requiring concentration • Fails to focus on details and/or makes thoughtless mistakes in schoolwork or assignments
Hyperactive/ Impulsive Type Diagnosis Criteria	**Hyperactive Symptoms:** • Squirms when seated or fidgets with feet/hands • Marked restlessness that is difficult to control • Appears to be driven by "a motor" or is often "on the go" • Lacks ability to play and engage in leisure activities in a quiet manner • Incapable of staying seated in class • Overly talkative **Impulsive Symptoms:** • Difficulty waiting turn • Interrupts or intrudes into conversations and activities of others • Impulsively blurts out answers before questions completed
Additional Requirements for Diagnosis	• Symptoms present prior to age 12 years • Symptoms not better accounted for by a different psychiatric disorder (e.g., mood disorder, anxiety disorder) and do not occur exclusively during a psychotic disorder (e.g., schizophrenia) • Symptoms not exclusively a manifestation of oppositional behavior
Classification	**Combined Type:** • Patient meets both inattentive and hyperactive/impulsive criteria for the past 6 months **Predominantly Inattentive Type:** • Patient meets inattentive criterion, but not hyperactive/impulse criterion, for the past 6 months **Predominantly Hyperactive/Impulsive Type:** • Patient meets hyperactive/impulse criterion, but not inattentive criterion, for the past 6 months Symptoms may be classified as mild, moderate, or severe based on symptom severity

Source: DSM-5 Diagnostic and Statistical Manual of Mental Disorders, 5th edition; ADHD: attention deficit hyperactivity disorder

Retrieved March 2, 2024, from: *adhd19-assessment-table1.pdf (aafp.org)*

Table 1
Demographic and Clinical Information of the ADHD (n = 400) Sample

Variable	Mean	SD
Age (years)	10.3	2.8
Grade	4.1	2.2
WISC-IV FSIQ	98.7	12.8

	Percent	Frequency
Diagnosis (%)		
ADHD-I	61.5	246
ADHD-C	38.5	154
Gender (%)		
Male	70.8	283
Female	29.3	117
School (%)		
Public	36.3	145
Private	63.8	255
Comorbid diagnoses (%)		
Reading disorder	26.8	107
Math disorder	14.3	57
Disorder of written expression	24.8	99
ODD	4.8	19
Anxiety disorder	7.5	30
Mood disorder	2.0	8
Adjustment disorder	22.8	91
Conduct disorder	0.5	2
Developmental coordination disorder (n = 71)	17.8	71
Expressive language disorder	7.3	29
Cannabis abuse	.5	4
Alcohol abuse	.4	3

Note. WISC-IV FSIQ = Wechsler Intelligence Scale for Children Full Scale IQ; ADHD-I = attention-deficit hyperactivity disorder predominantly inattentive type; ADHD-C = attention-deficit hyperactivity disorder combined type; ODD = oppositional defiant disorder.

In sum, it seems that the mere diagnosis (as seen in the chart above for diagnostic criteria measures) for ADHD, even in adulthood, may be too rigidly confined. Without considering dispositional factors for anxiety and relational constructs, this rigid structure of criteria may necessitate further revision to deconstruct (and re-construct) the DSM classification variables to include parental maltreatment measures, more concisely recognizing the potential underpinnings of ADHD pertinent to etiological effects. Not only will this give a clearer picture of the qualitatively defined concept of ADHD; it would also eliminate the requirement that ADHD *must* be present in childhood, as the current criteria "requires" for diagnosis, despite the age group measured.

In conclusion, it is purported that the rigid structure of criteria in the diagnosis for ADHD may heed consideration in the revision for its categorical limitations for ADHD; the research points to a deductive logical perspective in re-defining the features for labeling ADHD. In changing the criteria measures from the "requirement" that symptoms *must* be present in childhood, and by re-structuring the assessment criteria to include that of childhood maltreatment variables, a foundational new perspective emerges. Early experiences of abuse/neglect leading to maladaptive coping mechanisms as resultant predispositions for anxiety/depression subscales may better help to explain the manifestations of symptoms which constitute behavioral anomalies and better explain the late onset of ADHD in adulthood. It *can* be 'predisposed' by parental maltreatment in the forms of neglect and/or abuse; should attachment instability/insecurities re-occur in young adulthood years, during the critical phase of development when emotional regulation patterns characterize behavioral trends, underlying dispositional influences become important factors to consider. Attachment relationships harboring maladaptive trends may lead to the development of ADHD in adulthood, thus re-structuring the criteria measures to advocate the idea that ADHD *can* **develop** in **adulthood**.

Thus, within the context of psychology and psychiatry, mapping the theoretical framework onto the biological data, further exploring the developmental aspects breeds a new frontier in research and ultimately in practice: the newfound idea for Translational Developmental Psychobiology may be the breakthrough that has been sought for in research to this day; accounting for the predispositioned risk factors for inclusion in the structured criteria model thus helps to explain the variables to facilitate better understanding for the adult onset and development in the context of early risk factors and etiological constraints. In bridging the two disciplines of psychology in the conquest for mental health, this prospective view may help better explain the etiological significance for the development of adult ADHD; in doing so, a foundational new approach to diagnoses may undertake a pragmatic change, and therefore we may take a step forward in making changes by closing the translational gap.

X. References

*cover image: *Bloodflow Image May Help Clinicians Diagnose Bipolar Disorder*; August 22, 2013 (image: James Steidl/Shutterstock.com)

American Psychological Association, 2024 © (2018). APA Dictionary of Psychology [Electronic version]. *American Psychological Association*. Retrieved March 2, 2024, from *https://dictionary.apa.org/clinical-assessment.html*.

American Psychiatric Association. (2013). *Diagnostic and statistical manual of mental disorders* (5th ed.). Washington, DC: Author.

Bieleninik, L., Gradys, G., Dzhambov, A. M., Walczak,-Kozlowska, T., Lipowska, K; et al. (2023). Attention deficit in primary school-age children with attention deficit hyperactivity disorder measured with the attention network test: A systematic review and meta-analysis. *Frontiers in Neuroscience; Lausanne.* doi:10.3389/fnins.2023.1246490

Carlson, J. (2016). Clinical Assessment: Encyclopedia of Mental Health (Second Edition) [Electronic version]. *Academic Press,* 293-296.

Cupertino, R. B., Soheili-Nezhad, S., Grevet. E. H., Bandeira, C. E., Picon, F. A., Arauja Taveres, E., Naaijen, J., van Rooij, D., Akkermans, S., Vitols, E. S., Zweirs, M. P., Rovaris, D. L., Hoekstra, P. J., Breda, V., Oosterlaan, J., Hartman, C. A., Beckmann, C. F., Buitelaar, J. K., Franke, B., Dotto Bau, C. H., & Sprooten, E. (2020). Reduced fronto-striatal volume in attention-deficit/hyperactivity disorder in two cohorts across the lifespan [Electronic version]. *Neuroimage: Clinical, 28,* 1-9.

DSM-5 Diagnostic Criteria for ADHD (5th edition). [Electronic version]. *AAFP National Research Network.* Retrieved on March 3, 2024, from *https://www.aafp.org/dam/AAFP/documents/patient_care/adhd_toolkit/adhd19-assessment-table1.pdf?ref=clarityxdna.com*.

Edel, MA., Edel, S., Krüger, M. *et al.* Attachment, recalled parental rearing, and ADHD symptoms predict emotion processing and alexithymia in adults with ADHD. *Ann Gen Psychiatry* **14**, 43 (2015). Retrieved March 3, 2024, from *https://doi.org/10.1186/s12991-015-0082-y.html.*

Parke, E. M., Mayfield, A. R., Barchard, K. A., Thaler, N. S., Etcoff, L. M., & Allen, D. N. (2015). Factor structure of symptom dimensions in attention-deficit/hyperactivity disorder (ADHD). *Psychological Assessment, 27*(4), 1427–1437. https://doi.org/10.1037/pas0000121

Rosburg, T., von Allmen, D. Y., Langewitz, H., Weber, H., Bunker, E. B., & Langewitz, W. (2019). Patient-centeredness in psychiatric work disability evaluations and the reproducibility of work capacity estimates. *Patient Education and Counseling, 119,* 108093. Retrieved March 2, 2024, from *https://www.sciencedirect.com/science/article/pii/S0738399123004743.html.*

Moutsiana C, Fearon P, Murray L, Cooper P, Goodyer I, Johnstone T, & Halligan S. (2014). Making an effort to feel positive: insecure attachment in infancy predicts the neural underpinnings of emotion regulation in adulthood. *Journal of Child Psychol Psychiatry, 201455,* 999–1008.

Magai C. Affect, imagery, and attachment. In: Cassidy J, Shaver PR, editors. Handbook of attachment: theory, research, and clinical applications. *New York: Guilford Press;* 1999. p. 787–802.

Retz-Junginger P, Retz W, Blocher D, Weijers HG, Trott GE, Wender PH, et al. Wender Utah rating scale. The short-version for the assessment of the attention-deficit hyperactivity disorder (German). *Nervenarzt.* 2002; 73:830.

Stewart, R. E., & Chambless, D. L. (2009). Cognitive-behavioral therapy for adult anxiety disorders in clinical practice: A meta-analysis of effectiveness studies. *Journal of Consulting and Clinical Psychology, 77*(4), 595-606.

Grossman, A., & Avital, A. (2023). Emotional and sensory dysregulation as a possible missing link in attention deficit hyperactivity disorder: A review. *Frontiers in Behavioral Neuroscience; Lausanne.* doi: 10.3389/fnbeh.2023.1118937

Pangambam, S. Transcript: Stanford's Robert Sapolsky on Depression in U.S. (Full Lecture). (2016). *The Singju Post. Education.* Retrieved on March 4, 2024, from *https://rediscoveringsacredness.com/wp-content/uploads/2019/01/attachment-styles.jpg.*

Rosack, J. (2004). Brain Scans Reveal Physiology of ADHD. *Psychiatric News, 39*(1). Published Online:2 Jan 2004. Retrieved on March 4, 2024, from *https://doi.org/10.1176/pn.39.1.0026*

Steidl, J. (2013). Blood-Flow Measure May Help Clinicians Diagnose Bipolar Disorder [Electronic version]. Retrieved on February 18, 2023, from *https://www.bing.com/images/search?view=detailV2&ccid=5ZHeaIW1&id=39CACE2E056411D8 5899A8F2DC73D36FD7F93FBF&thid=OIP.5ZHeaIW1goqjs-wNGHq2TgAAAA&mediaurl=https%3a%2f%2f2.bp.blogspot.com*

Text citation: (American Psychiatric Association, 2013). Retrieved on March 2, 2024, from **(http:www.ons.gov.uk/peoplepopulationandcommunity/crimeandjustice/methodologies/userguidetocr imestatisticsforenglandandwales)*

*DSM-5 Diagnostic Criteria for ADHD; retrieved March2, 2024, from *https://www.aafp.org/dam/AAFP/ documents/patient_care/adhd_toolkit/adhd19-assessment-table1.pdf?ref=clarityxdna.com adhd19-assessment-table1.pdf (aafp.org)*

ABOUT THE AUTHOR

Amy M. Twilegar is a post-graduate student, recently completing her Data Analytics and Visualization Boot Camp through UC Davis. She graduated from UC Davis with her Bachelor of Science degree from UC Davis in 2009, followed by earning her Master's degree in Psychology from the University of the Rockies in Colorado in 2013. Having completed her Data Analytics and Visualization Boot Camp in 2022, she has gone on to publish her works in this book, and aspires to getting her Ph.D. and become a professor in the newly introduced field of Translational Developmental Psychobiology. With her independent research newly published, she is eager and looking forward to her next pursuits in education, and one day leave a footprint having made a great difference in this world. As a research assistant at San Jose State University and research associate as well as co-editor at Stanford University, she embarks on her arduous journey to becoming a great asset to the psychological research community, and looks forward to every step of the way.

Printed in the United States
by Baker & Taylor Publisher Services